PIMP MY SKULLS

Sugar Skulls Coloring Book

70+ UNIQUE IMAGES

- BOOKS REVOLUTION -

THESE ARE JUST SOME OF THE BEAUTIFUL IMAGES YOU WILL FIND IN THIS BOOK..

.. NOT THE USUAL SUGAR SKULLS IMAGES

70+ UNIQUE & AWESOME SUGAR SKULL

COLORING IMAGES INSIDE

RESEARCH SHOW THAT COLORING CALMS ANXIETY.

SUGAR SKULL IS THE PERFECT SUBJECT TO FOCUS YOUR
MIND AND RELEASE YOUR IMAGINATION.

CONGRATULATION!

YOU CAN START RELAXING BY COLORING OUR BEAUTIFUL
AND INTRICATELY SUGAR SKULL ILLUSTRATION

THIS COLORING BOOK BELONG TO

....

....

....

....

....

....

....

....

....

....

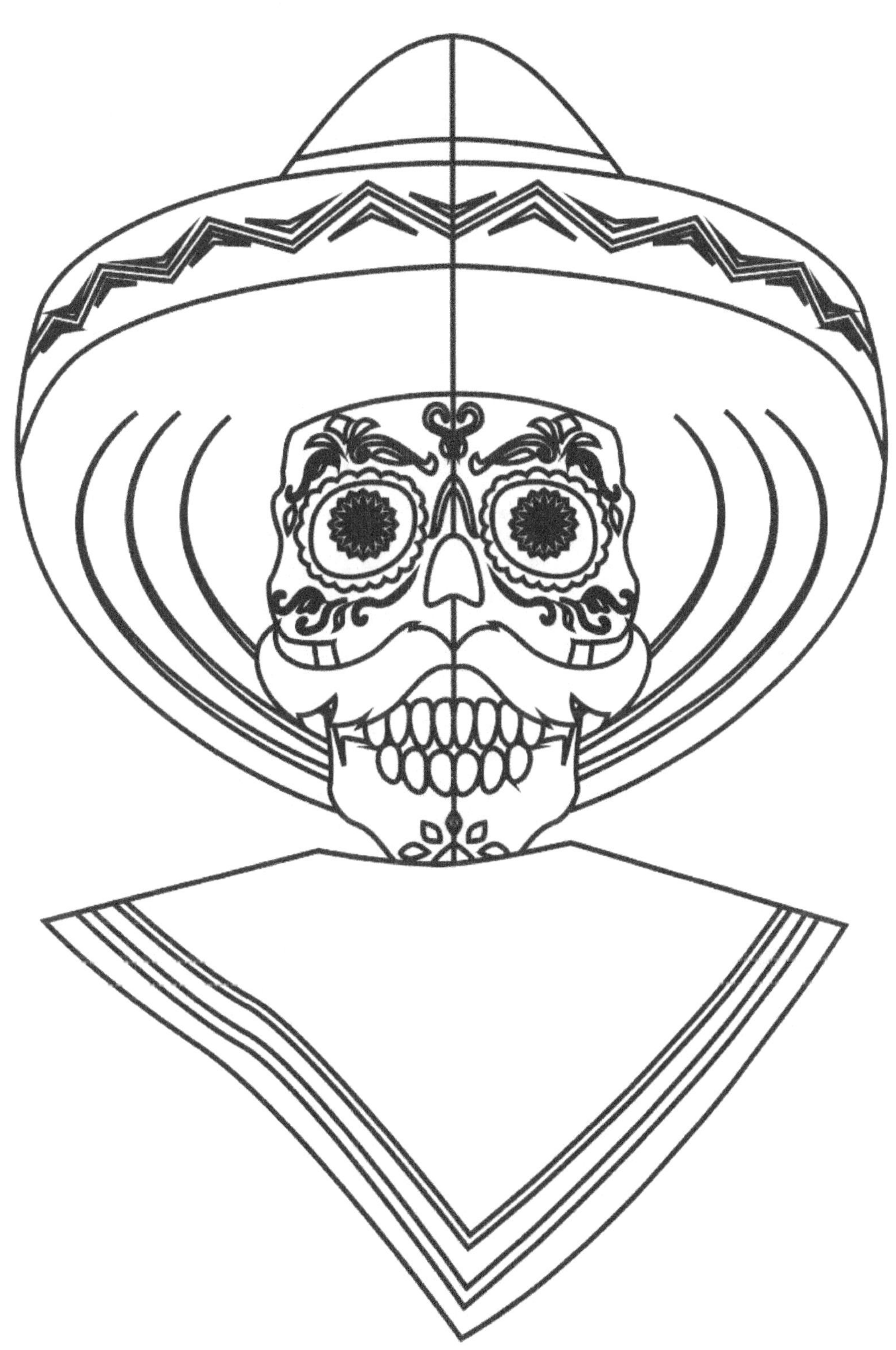

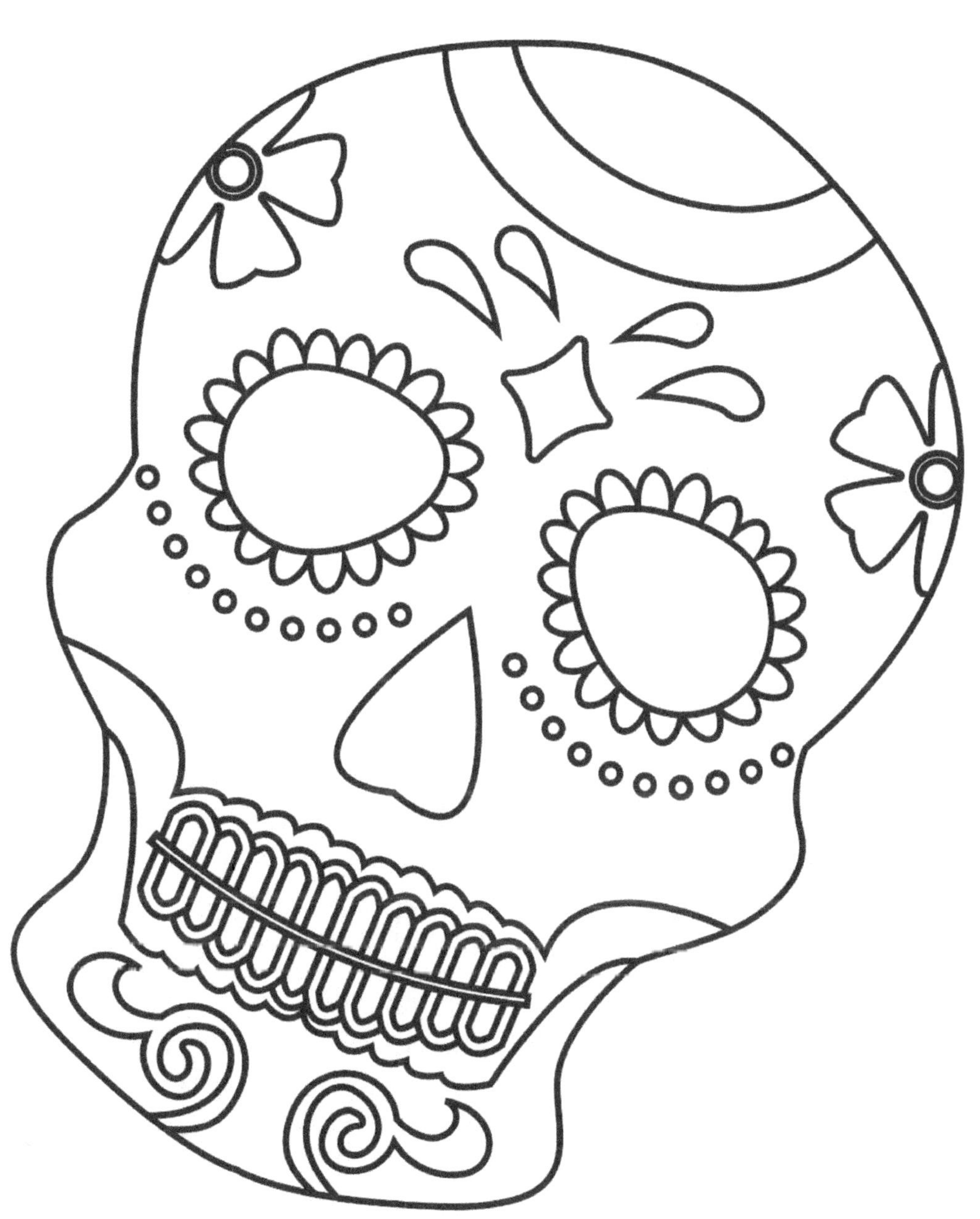

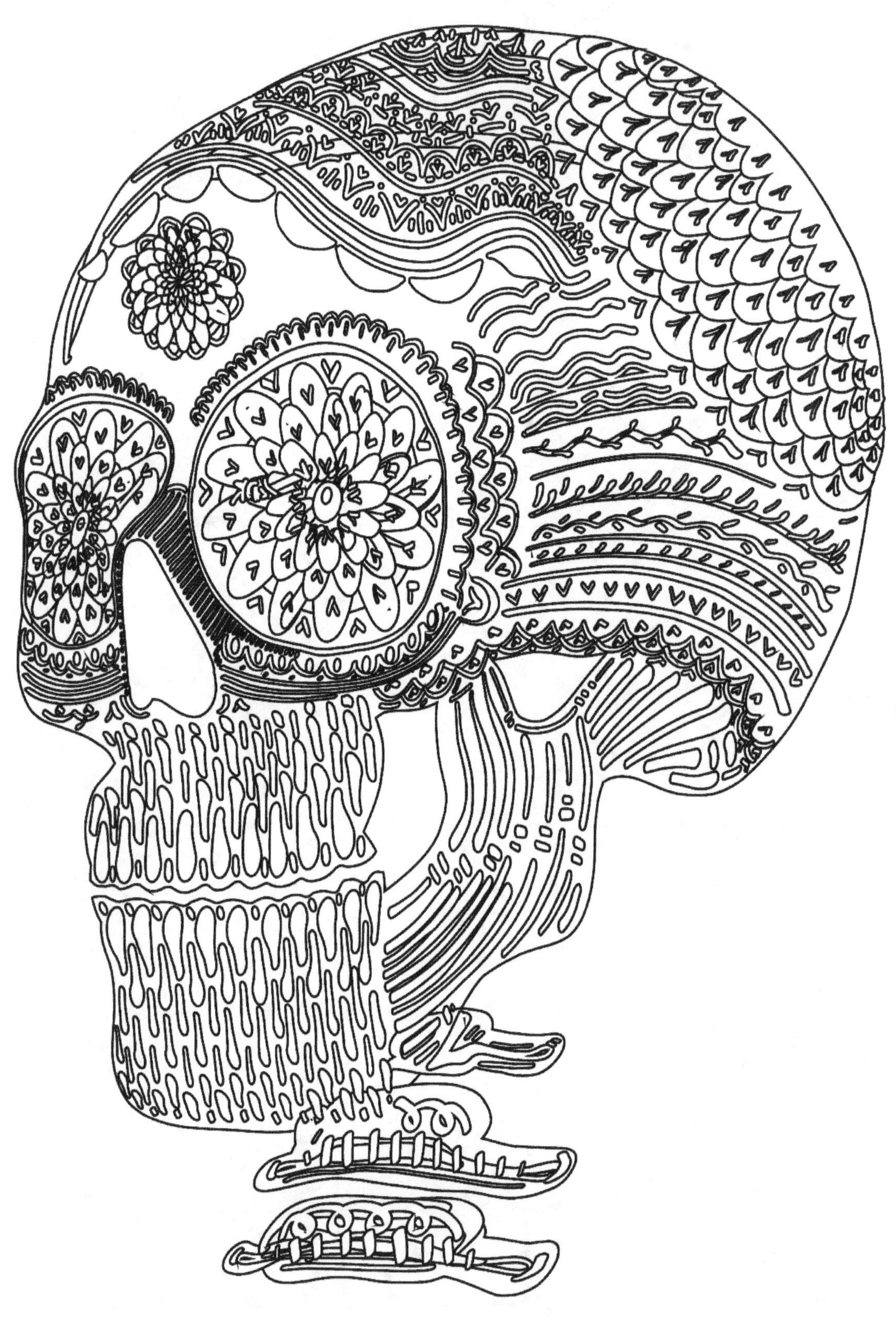

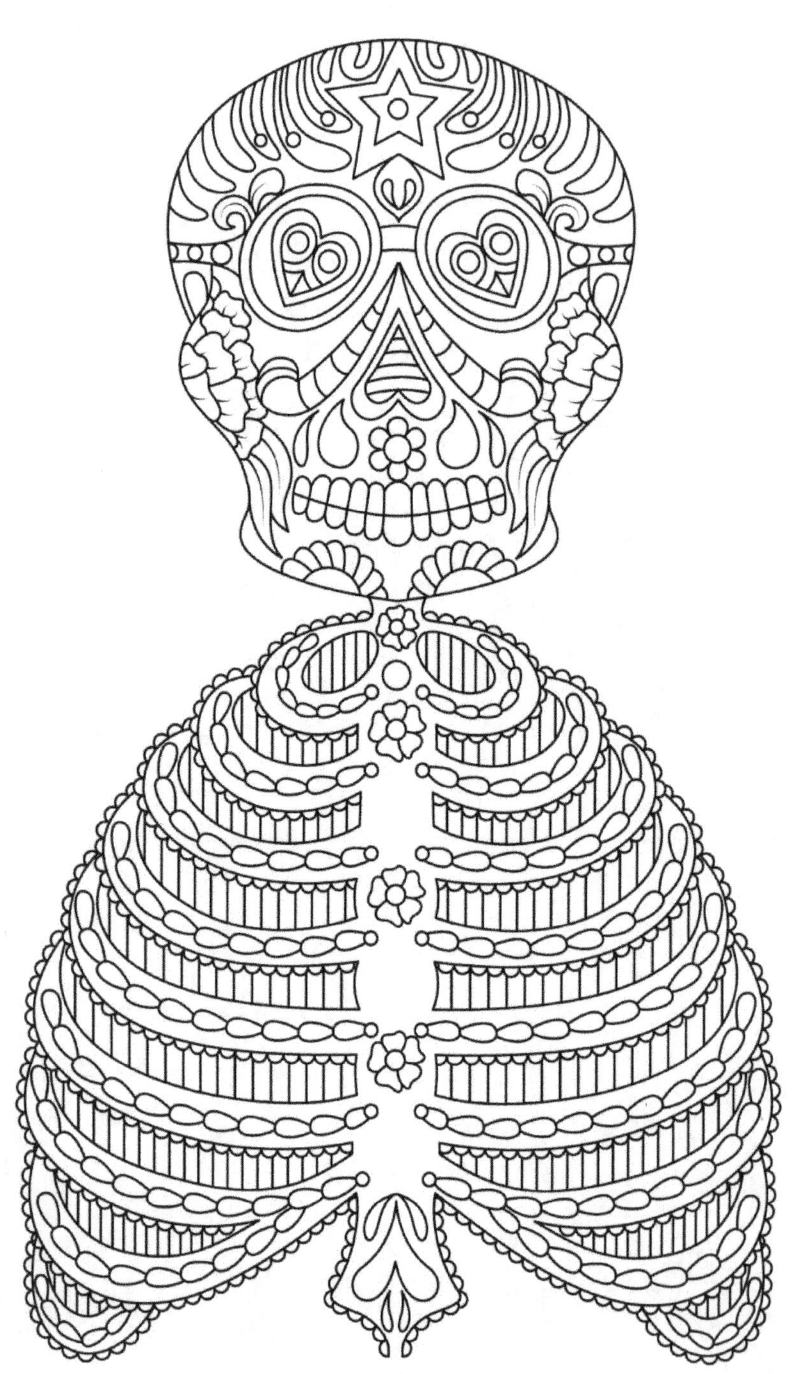